Engineering Thermodynamics
Work and Heat Transfer

By the same authors
*Thermodynamic and Transport Properties
of Fluids (SI Units)*, 4th edn (Basil Blackwell)
*Diagram for Temperature Rise versus Fuel–Air Ratio for Combustion
of a Gas Turbine Fuel* (Basil Blackwell)

By H. Cohen, G. F. C. Rogers and H. I. H. Saravanamuttoo
Gas Turbine Theory, 5th edn (Pearson)

By G. F. C. Rogers
The Nature of Engineering (Macmillan)

By Y. R. Mayhew
'Conventions and nomenclature for physical quantities,
units, numbers and mathematics', chapter in *Heat
Exchanger Design Handbook* (Begell House, 1994)

Contents